CAIN

Luke Kennard has published five collections of poetry. He won an Eric Gregory Award in 2005 and was shortlisted for the Forward Prize for Best Collection in 2007. He lectures at the University of Birmingham. In 2014 he was selected by the Poetry Book Society as one of the Next Generation Poets. His debut novel, *The Transition*, is published in 2017 by Fourth Estate.

ALSO BY LUKE KENNARD

POETRY

The Solex Brothers (Stride, 2005)
The Harbour Beyond the Movie (Salt Publishing, 2007)
The Migraine Hotel (Salt Publishing, 2009)
Planet-Shaped Horse (Nine Arches Press, 2011)
The Necropolis Boat (Holdfire, 2011)
A Lost Expression (Salt Publishing, 2012)

FICTION

Holophin (Penned in the Margins, 2012)

Cain

Luke Kennard

Penned in the Margins

LONDON

PUBLISHED BY PENNED IN THE MARGINS
Toynbee Studios, 28 Commercial Street, London E1 6AB
www.pennedinthemargins.co.uk

First published 2016

Printed in the United Kingdom by CPI Group Ltd.

ISBN
978-1-908058-35-5

CONTENTS

ACKNOWLEDGEMENTS

Best British Poetry 2015 (Salt Publishing, 2015), *The Learned Pig, Poetry London, Poetry* (Chicago), *BODY, The Poet's Quest for God* (Eyewear, 2015). Thanks to all editors.

I am indebted to the poet Gregory Betts, who first introduced me to the long-form anagram when I told him I was working on poems about Cain. His collection *If Language* was a major influence and catalyst. I am equally grateful to Dr Crystal Bennes, whose initial belief in the project, encouragement and advice on sequencing was invaluable, and who also provided the form for the scholia.

I.M. John Cashin

Cain

Like Cain, we are condemned, o wretched soul, for we have offered to the Creator of all only our defiled actions, a polluted sacrifice and a useless life.

THE CANON OF ST ANDREW OF CRETE

LUCIFER: Poor clay! / And thou pretendest to be wretched! Thou!

BYRON, *CAIN*

Try persuading the world not to cut its own throat for half a decade or more, like me, under one name or another, and it'll begin to dawn on you that even *your* behaviour's part of its plan.

MALCOLM LOWRY, *UNDER THE VOLCANO*

BOOK I

GRAVEL PIT

Cain's Prologue

That you were *marked* all scholars can agree
but where, how, why and if it worked presents
the reader some perplexity. A mark
for humiliation or protection?
For you or others? Their first untouchable.
So Philo has as *immortality*
what others thought a tremor or a shake.
St Ambrose has death postponed in mercy
to fashion you infinite time to repent;
St Jerome as punishment to have you
witness generations of hardship.
Artists gave you the curse of beardlessness,
c.f. Judas Iscariot, the smooth,
the bare-faced liar, the androgynous
enchanter. But artists also gave you hair
beyond hair, a hirsute, shaggy brute such that
Lamech, the short-sighted hunter, might
have taken you for a beast:
I have slain a man to my wounding and
a young man to my hurt — he won't say who.
For others you are still around today,
eternal wanderer somewhere in Tennessee,
a vampire so bored he seeks death.
Tutelary spirit of the fugitive and
heavenly advocate for fan fiction:
Targum, Pseudo-Jonathan, Midrashim.

I prefer your stammer, your constant nod
many mistake for compliance
(an embarrassingly literal scholar's
interpretation of The Land of Nod).
A dowsing-rod shake to your arms
or a single horn, or horn-like lump.
In an uncanonical Armenian Adambook
the horn can speak. A single horn
screaming: *Here comes Cain, the murderer!*
(How a horn speaks I don't know —
maybe like a beak?) Tent-dwelling pastoralist
or the city-builder whose every house
collapses on his head. Lyre and pipe-player,
patron saint of oases and mirages,
eponymous ancestor of the Kenites,
a nomadic tribe of smiths who marked
themselves with their own tools:
the first tattoo. Our Lady of Hidden Agendas,
Oh Father of Human Resources,
Tertullian has you as another fallen angel,
but give us the comfort of intentional distortions,
doulos, slave, unintended consequences,
the first godfather, the first dogwalker,
the first cussed, first touched,
the successful, happy killer God does not punish;
gun runner, human trafficker, the sun
shines upon you, the sun shines upon you,
may the sun shine upon you.

A Stranger's Disaster

When I lost my faith and my marriage in the same week my friends
    said: that's ok, we never believed in the construct of
    romantic love, the redundant institution of marriage and
    the state-sponsored mental self-abuse of religion anyway.
    Welcome to the 21st century, asshole.
So I sought comfort in wine-strength wheat beers which tasted of
    childhood medicine. I bought an Amiga 600 on eBay and
    player-managed Luton Town to the top of the Premiership
    in Sensible World of Soccer, the grunt and whir of the 3.5"
    save-disk, the matte of its torn fuzzy label sticker on
    my fingertips, the smell of dust cooked on the hot beige
    plastic transformer.
I Tweeted things like: 'Kids, you think TV is pretty great, but let
    me tell you about TV and alcohol! You got so much to look
    forward to!'
I grew an unconvincing beard.
I took two weeks' compassionate leave then switched to Laphroaig
    in my coffee and gave lectures about Imagism and
    the Beats where my voice was like a distant siren
    rushing to a stranger's disaster; I sympathised with
    Extenuating Circumstances and between seminars I cried
    in a small disused classroom on the 5th floor because I
    missed my children.
Someone had started making these humiliating video collages of
    me which bothered me more than it ought to have done in
    the circumstances.

At night I imagined I was a drone pilot flying over his own shack,
 a finger hovering above the A button. Under my direction
 Luton Town won the European Championship.
I became something not-human. A bad headache or some ideology.
 None of this means anything. Let's do all we can to prolong
 it. Some municipal flotsam persisting in the villages.

No Wait Come Back I Want to Tell You About

this DDoS attack on my heart
this giant gravel bag
this constant, gentle renunciation of love
this rain on the cliff face
this roll of the eyes
this instant decaf
this dead pigeon

This DDoS Attack on My Heart

one common method of attack involves
saturating the target mechanism
with external communications requests
so much so that it cannot respond to legitimate traffic
or responds so slowly
as to be rendered essentially unavailable.

Enter Cain

Doorbell sounds its overeager quiz.
An actual size, inflatable Frankenstein's monster
is propped on my doorstep.
I have a pin in my hand. I stick it in.
Blam. Behind it stands Cain,
his beard blocking out the sun.
'How did you know I'd have a pin?'
'I thought you'd either be hovering
over a world map or taking up the hem
of your trousers,' says Cain. 'Which?'
'I was removing a photo of my ex-wife
from the kitchen noticeboard.'
'Ah,' says Cain. 'The trouble is you
have to live with every decision you make.'
He presents his papers. *This is Cain.*
Everyone is very concerned about you.
We have sent him to make sure you don't do
anything stupud. 'Stupud?' 'Probably a typo,'
Cain says. 'It's probably meant to say stupid.'

Painted Dream-Bird (I Wanted to Send a Message)

I have found 10 of your nail varnishes:
Glottal Stop; The Fog; School of Quietude;
Gold Fiction; Tangerine; Tsundoku
Bellyflop; Colossal Overreaction; Pill Pink;
Bright Blue Redundant; Wrong Kind of Party.
I arrange them around me on the desk
in a semicircle and under a sad dog lamp
I paint each of my fingernails, meticulous
as a man restoring his Warhammer figurines.
'I think the trouble is you're trying to fight
the sadness,' says Cain. 'That's like trying
to steer out of the skid: intuitive, understandable
but completely unhelpful. You steer *into*
the skid, you regain control. Perverse, but...'
He gives me a paper wallet of photos of you
at university which I have never seen before.
There are very few photos of you at university
because digital cameras didn't exist,
but some people had a 35mm camera
from Argos and it cost £17 to develop 24 photos
and most of them had thumbs in.
In the photos you are playing a guitar,
you are in a production of *The Seagull*,
you are at parties in dresses I don't know.
In the photos your face wears several expressions
you don't make anymore and I know I've destroyed

everything about you which first drew me to you.
Cain pours me a strong coffee, a glass of red wine.

Artificial Signs

When you are very hungover
your brain is a metaphor, your face is a prawn.
You should go to a part of town which is also in pain:
cash converters, betting shops, cash converters,
betting shops, cash converters, betting shops.

Cain buys me a yellow fairy cake with a purple
monster ring embedded in the icing.
First he puts it on my ring finger,
then he says he hates it and throws it in the stunted hedge.
Some retro cans and unfoiled crisp packets.

~

Cain takes me to Sunningdale, an old people's home where he
        volunteers.
I don't know what to say to anyone.
Cain goes around the rec room asking people how they're doing.
I try to do the same.
I ask the man nearest me how he is doing.
He tells me that he wants to blow his nose.
I go to look for an employee.

~

'While I'm here it's probably best that I get to know you,'

Cain says. 'We'll talk about some formative experiences,
your fears, frustrations, memories, blocks.
You might even get a poem out of it, eh?'

'Fuck off.'

The supermarket's logo is resplendent in the twilight.
When I scan the first bottle the automated checkout says
Approval needed and Cain says, 'She really *gets* you.'

Balcony

Listen: as a child I thought of being a soldier
in the Devil's army, vanquished in the last battle,
ceasing to exist, and nothing forever.

An angel killed me and then there was nothing.
No dark or light element to silently float in,
no element; no floating; no subject or object:
no soft barometer to register the nothing.
No critics of the neither abject nor beautiful nothing.

Like fastening a necklace you aren't wearing;
trying to soothe a looped recording of a crying baby;
like lighting a fire with the wood you chopped in a game.

But if I concentrated, I could feel it,
before I knew the words *infinity* or *oblivion*.

It does not end or begin; there is no outside of it, or if there is
that is where we are now briefly perched.
We play with toy cars or lounge about smoking on a very

privileged loggia. And then I thought:
I am lucky to have put away such unforgiving fantasies,
but then I thought now for a certainty this is the only balcony.

Fridge Magnet

Cain says, 'You're sad. Here.'
He gives me a fridge magnet of a kitty.
A Russian Blue wearing a wizard's cape.

The kitty is saying:

You are not fertiliser. Your soul is to be archived.
Oh, you who doesn't even question electricity.
The dreams where you're flying are not dreams.

It adheres to my fridge as if relieved.
I take out a bottle of Sancerre, a hard cheese.

Vestigial Stammer

As a child I stammered. It took me from the age of 13 to 17
to finish the sentence I- I- I- I- I- I- I- I- I- I- I- I- I- I-.
But now my stammer only comes back when I have to say my own
        name.
There is a chasm between Luke and Kennard.
There is a pause like a cat weighing up its chances
at making a jump before I manage to say 'Luke' in Starbucks.
(Cain suggests an ostentatious fake name, but I can't).

I look this up online to see if anyone else gets it.
They do. If you can rephrase what you're trying to say,
if you can find a synonym (this is how my vocabulary
developed), you work around the blockage; the car snicks
by the accident and speeds off down the closed lane.
I still stammer when, and only when, I have to say my name
because there is nothing else for it.

'That, and because you hate yourself,' says Cain.

Birds/Trees

Some things I love to take for granted, but
other people get really interested in them.
Cain is always reading books about birds or trees.
'Why are you so interested in trees, Cain?' I'll ask him.
Or, if he's reading a book about birds, I'll say,
'Why are you so interested in birds, Cain?'
And he'll say, 'It's what we've got.
Seems sensible to take an interest, no?'

Self-Portrait at Primary School

I was so obliging I let the weirdest, smelliest kid pick on me
because I thought it might make him feel better.
He smelled like an opened can. They called him the weirdo.

Instead of the red sweatshirt with the school logo on the right
       breast,
he had a generic red jumper which wasn't even the right shade of
       red.

I remember the grain of the wood on the prefab classroom's base
against my scalp as he gently, then firmly, rolled my head against
       it.
I remember the rolling turned to knocking, a tuft of my hair in his
       fist.

I didn't say: *Don't do that because that hurts me.* I didn't
want to hurt his feelings. I remember smiling quizzically at him
and he beamed back, delighted with this human doll.

The relationship continued for a week until a dinner lady
marched us both to my teacher. The Weirdo was sent for
       counselling
and never allowed to go near me again.

And even at the time it struck me: maybe I was the dangerous one.

On Being Very Annoying

See because looking back the wonder is that I wasn't picked on a lot more. I was a terrible sportsman. I mean no shit, right? Poet has inferiority complex: stop the presses. I had an anti-talent for all sports. There were two five-a-side courts and we had the one on the left. The whole male population of the yeargroup, around 50 kids, would play 25-aside at break and lunchtime. From above it must have looked like a boiling pan. How I longed for the ball to stick on the chicken wire and burst. This happened once and the game carried on a minute or two with a popped leather shell until even the most dedicated gave up and punted it over the wall and we stood around in clusters talking for the rest of break. Heaven. So anyway, because I basically couldn't play, I would go around being annoying. That's not self-deprecation or a consequence of my personality: I had every intention of being annoying. It's like I was going for a Grade 5 in *being annoying*. It was how I passed the time. I had fictional advertising agencies in my head and a variety of profoundly irritating voices engaged in stories which had whole plot arcs and lasted weeks, months. Three years of this. Year 8, year 9, year 10. A half-hour morning break and a one-hour lunch break. Every weekday. Three years. I didn't have the nous to think: I don't fit in here at all. I should be playing Dungeons & Dragons or out past the fence with the smokers. That's alarmingly passive, isn't it? You're in an untenable situation and instead of doing the slightest thing to change it you turn into some kind of gibbering outsider who satirises everything around him while never leaving the confines of his own imagination, here represented by the chicken wire fence, *but you don't leave.* There were so many players that everyone spent quite a lot of time off the ball, so I had plenty of space to come up with my extemporisations. Monologues, multiple character scenes, fake product placement. I targeted the boys just barely higher than me on the social pecking order. I subjected them to excruciating logorrhea: a hellish Total Theatre where the actor pursues you after you've walked out. I'd get in the way of the occasional pass or shot. How I plagued them. And all they'd give me back was a kind of resigned entreaty: *Please go away! Please shut up! Please! Kennard, for fuck's sake!* The occasional dead arm when they were really exasperated. It was a form of love.

Intermezzo Zolpimist

Sometimes I think this will all go away
if I can find the right combination
of caffeine, alcohol and misfortune.
The auto-reject is held in another tab.
Someone tricked you into taking
yourself seriously. I don't feel this ever
passing: my friend is a nurse and she says
it doesn't ever pass and I trust her.
I watch the cogs from the motorway bridge,
and help is a publicity stunt
and talking about it is cold water.
Stepping into a river in my best shoes.
I think *that's apt* and then I feel sick.
Back at the glass eye museum, Cain
takes my hand. 'You're as bad as science,'
he says. 'I wish the philosophers
would get involved again.'

Proof of the Soul #1

'Come on,' says Cain. 'Come on. We're going for a walk.
Stop you moping around the house. I'm going to prove
to you that the soul exists.' I pull my laces until my feet
throb. We walk towards the mouldy pub I like.

Within five minutes we fall in some way behind
a young woman in a white sundress embroidered with
little black skulls and yellow triangles.
'You like her, don't you? Stare at her,' says Cain.

'Drink her in. Stare. Imagine you are a scanner
and you are trying to scan her. Keep looking…'
Every cell in my body mainlines a badly dated sitcom.
We are walking along and I am staring and I

convert her movements into currency.
The service not the goods — that's where the margins
are. I am about to look away or at my feet
when she glances over her shoulder, reproachfully.

I gasp as our eyes lock like people offering condolences.
I feel humiliated. I want to say *I'm sorry I'm not like that*
which is a lie and anyway all of this takes place in 0.2 of a second.
She walks on as Cain and I cross the road.

'There,' he says. 'There. Your souls were in full communion.
Invisibly, miraculously. Hers was saying: *Leave me alone.*'
Later in a café with mirrored windows Cain indicates
a near-spherical man tottering on a bicycle.

I stare at him, disgusted. He looks directly at me through the
        mirror:
an expression of intense worry, wobbles, nearly comes off the bike.
'Do souls say anything other than leave me alone?' I ask.
'In my experience?' says Cain. 'No.'

Ehyeh Asher Ehyeh

Cain takes me on a pilgrimage to a shrine. This place is amazing, he says. You have to stand for a long time and then a man with a long beard and such love in his eyes they are all pupil, they burn like the furnace of an old hotel and you know that he sees exactly who and what you are, but loves you anyway, he anoints you with oil and then there's a feast and the women and the men are beautiful and they talk to you as if you are too. And the *food*! And the *wine*! I mean, I won't drink much because I'm driving, but honestly, Kennard, you're going to love this. He drives me four hours into the countryside. The grey trees are haggard, subaqueous. We abandon the car once the road peters out under hanging branches. Waves crash against the dark cliff face. We walk the narrow ridge for miles, supporting ourselves on long sticks which reach the thinner bank below. When I lose mine it fades to a splinter. Without it I bruise my fingers hanging to the side. Here we are, says Cain, at last. But what's left of the shrine is gagged with weeds and vines, a crumbled sundial, half the flagstones pouring into the sea, a slice of monkey temple from a childhood textbook. Wrong century, says Cain. Sorry. Anyway, let's head home. I've set you up on a date.

All of Which Was Maybe Too Much to Go into on Our First Social Engagement, But I Felt Like We Had an Affinity

You're as bad as the last Unitarian I dated. I'm trying
to tell you how the water feels: a network of cities in the brain.

But you think the wide-mouthed vat of miracles pours as copious
on the prefab shack of school chairs / the cathedral 800 died
      raising.

At the wishing-well's margin you wish for disappointment, I wish
that the opposite of coffee existed and then I think in the 18th
      century

we would meet in a gravel pit to discuss the Psalms because that
      was the least
consecrated place we could think of: a gravel pit! The ever-
      changing, shingly surface;

our thin soles; hum of rudimentary machines; fine sand in our
      nostrils
coagulating into a toxic paste; occasional stab of flint or an elbow…

Because a king is a tyrant or a keyring novelty,
because a lord is a landowner with a lifetime peerage,

What should we rename our god? The sound a PC makes
when you switch it off? Three things: I'm sorry for your loss;

your scarf is pretty; I'd like to take you somewhere far away
where the air is more delightfully opaque. I know

I am the heart's estate agent. I know the cuffs of my trousers
trail unholy water wherever we go. I know. I know. I know.

Proof of the Soul #2

A priest is asked to perform an exorcism — a rite he has never been called upon to execute in his entire clerical career — on a perfectly affable middle-aged man who appears to be suffering no symptoms or effects of demonic possession. They said they had to ask someone High Church, says Donna. Don't disappoint them. It's two nights. Why not go? It'll be a good story. When the priest arrives the man is cutting brambles back from a rose bush in the front garden. Good morning. Ah, thank you for coming at such short notice, Father. Not at all. The priest finds nothing wrong with him, but the man's family insist that he requires exorcism. His wife, their teenage son, his visiting sister. Father, thank you for coming to us. They have the touching, bovine look of a family standing in the hard shoulder next to their totalled car. The priest is used to seeing people in this state. So has he been acting... strangely? Is he under an unusual amount of stress? Have they seen a doctor? Both women close their eyes. We're just really glad you're here, says the son. But the man himself is cheerful, busies himself making tea. Or would you rather coffee? Just instant, I'm afraid. But the tea is leaf tea. Thought so. The house is a detached, sensitively modernised property in a

(In secret.) Help me help

peaceful part of town. 'A leafy suburb' you might call it if you're the kind of person who can give voice to such platitudes without feeling as though you're suffocating in your own words. He is not. He accepts a tumbler of brandy before bed, an expensive-looking tumbler which is trying very hard to be spherical. The man chats about his paintings, which are all of men fishing. The priest is shown up to his room: it is the half of the attic which has not been converted into a study. A large bed with goosedown bedding to which he is too polite to admit he's mildly allergic. On the wall there is an icon, in the Byzantine style, of Jonah being swallowed by the whale, but the whale looks more like some kind of red, scaly sea monster with snaggleteeth. The priest makes the sign of the cross, says his evening prayers with compunction and gets into bed. And also much cattle, he mutters. The priest does not like being away from home and does not like being a guest — this is probably a form of pride, he thinks. Unusually, the priest sleeps well. In the morning he meets the woman on the landing. I'm sorry. There doesn't seem to be anything wrong with your husband at all. It may be best if I leave you good people to it. She stares at him until he says, but maybe I should stay to see how today goes. At breakfast he asks the man whether *he* believes he requires exorcism and the man smiles as he pours the tea. Oh yes,

me help me help me help
me help me help me help
me help me help me help
me help me help me help
me help me help me help
me help me help me help
me help me help me help
me help me help me help
me help me help me help
me help me help me help
me help me help me help
me help me help me help
me help me help me help
me help me help me help
me help me help me help
me help me help me help
me help me help me help
me help me help me help
me help me help me help
me help me help me help
me help me help me help
me help me help me help
me help me help me help
me help me help me help
me help me help me help
me help me help me help
me help me help me help
me help me help me help
me help me help me help
me help me help me help
me help me help me help
me help me help me help
me help me help me help
me help me help me help
me help me help me help
me help me help me help

certainly. Sooner the better. By this point I'm more demon than man. But what is his evidence? Evidence? The man whistles. Yes, evidence. On what grounds do he and his family believe that he needs to be exorcised? It is funny that he should use the word 'ground.' It is? Yes. Funny. And why is that? Because we place such faith in the ground we walk on, don't we? Oh, but he meant grounds as in proof. Ah. Well, we could get started if you like? Oh no, Father, sorry. Could we... He suddenly seems very tired and irritable. Could we not perhaps do this... tonight instead? Of course. That's fine. In your own time. The priest tries the son. What made you call me? What has your father done? The boy sighs and closes his laptop. Here's a very short analogy. Last year my mate trained as a tattoo artist, and I'd always thought about getting a tattoo, so when it came to him needing human subjects to practise on, I stepped up. He was going to do a tiger on the back of my shin in, like, a calligraphy style. Took ages, hurt more than I thought it would. But check out the results. The boy rolls up the right leg of his black skinny jeans and presents the back of his shin. The words *KEEP STILL, DAMMIT!* are tattooed on his calf in uneven letters. I see. Do you? Not sure *I* do. Outside the priest finds the aunt sitting in a deck chair. She is wearing a large floppy hat. She is drinking tea. About your brother, says the priest. He was always

me help me help me help
me help me help me help
me help me help me help
me help me help me help
me help me help me help
me help me help me help
me help me help me help
me help me help me help
me help me help me help
me help me help me help
me help me help me help
me help me help me help
me help me help me help
me help me help me help
me help me help me help
me help me help me help
me help me help me help
me help me help me help
me help me help me help
me help me help me help
me help me help me help
me help me help me help
me help me help me help
me help me help me help
me help me help me help
me help me help me help
me help me help me help
me help me help me help
me help me help me help
me help me help me help
me help me help me help
me help me help me help
me help me help me help
me help me help me help

a very kind man, she says. And now? Now, to be quite honest, I just wish he would die. The priest is perturbed. He seems perfectly nice to me. She almost scoffs, but corrects herself. With respect, Father, you've only just met him. That night the priest stands next to his heavy black case. The man sits in his armchair, smiling. His wife, son and sister are sitting on the sofa, hunched forwards. You all seem absolutely determined, so I'm going to go through with this anyway, but I want to warn you: it is dangerous to mock that which we do not understand. It would be very foolish to do this as some kind of joke or out of idle curiosity. It is my opinion that there is nothing wrong with this man, and I hope the performance of the rite will not be at great personal cost to me or to you. I am doing this in good faith. The priest looks up at the ceiling as he says this, but it is not a conscious appeal to God and nor is he rolling his eyes in exasperation, although it could be taken for either (and is, in fact) and the proximity of the two gestures/facial expressions has never struck him until now although Christ, he has always liked to think, rolled his eyes quite a lot: *How much longer must I... Well neither will I tell you on whose authority... You couldn't watch for one hour?* And actually — and he feels this with the absolute conviction of a chemical symbol — actually every single thing you say and do is a prayer, regardless of your feelings on the matter.

me help me help me help
me help me help me help
me help me help me help
me help me help me help
me help me help me help
me help me help me help
me help me help me help
me help me help me help
me help me help me help
me help me help me help
me help me help me help
me help me help me help
me help me help me help
me help me help me help
me help me help me help
me help me help me help
me help me help me help
me help me help me help
me help me help me help
me help me help me help
me help me help me help
help me help me help me

Attracted by a Black Hole

Cain suggests a change of tack.
'I've got you a reading in a tent at a literary festival,'
he says, peeling a banana and taking a bite of peel.
Might want to work on some new material.'
Why? I say. Why would I want to work on some
new material? 'I think you're in a good place.'
Why can't I just do some old material?
'Yes, well I mean why not?' says Cain.
'You could be the only villager who brings
a jug of water for the Empress's enchanted milk
bath assuming the night will shield your stinginess,
but then the sun will rise and it will turn out,
to your horror, that everyone had the same idea
and the pool is full of water. And the King
will put you all to death for the hardness of your hearts.'

Tarp

Squeak of the big wheel, squall of feedback
from the unpopular poetry tent. Cain
said I was on the bill but I'm not.
He tells me to lie down. I feel the lumpy field
beneath the sackcloth mould to my back.
He covers me with a heavy woven blanket,

proceeds around me with his long, flat-headed nails,
his wooden mallet bristly with overuse.
'Tappy-tappy-tappy,' he says as he works.
I cannot move my legs nor then my arms.
It crushes half the air from my lungs.
I crane my neck. 'Why are you doing this?'

'To demonstrate to you that even a book festival
can become the site of an atrocity,' says Cain.
'That's completely inane,' I protest, writhing.
'Even a platitude is transfigured by violence.'
He stretches the blanket over my head like a caul,
I feel my nose crack as the nails tap. I stop breathing.

Zombies

When I come round everyone is *big* into zombies:
they are playing zombie games and watching big-budget
remakes of zombie films. They dress up as zombies
and spend half the day in SFX getting made up to look
more like zombies. They go on zombie team-building exercises,
They have zombie-themed weddings and read
zombie comic books and watch many episodes of high quality
zombie dramas. It's like I've died and gone to stupid.

'What's the deal with zombies?' I ask a man
dressed as a zombie in one of many *Ask a Zombie*
booths which have popped up on the high street.
'We're having a zombie moment,' he says.
'Clearly zombies have tapped into some key
part of the collective unconscious I don't have
because I do not give a flying fuck about zombies,'
I tell him. 'Easy there, buddy,' he says.
'You looked at yourself recently?'

Television Knows No Night

Oh open window, oh immobility of Nature,
oh spectacle of emotional magniloquence,
oh error about life entirely necessary, oh
Miltonic angels of the subchannel, oh
aspect ratio I'd love you but would fade away,
oh bitrate of energy and spirit oh,
copyrighted catastrophic legions, I found
myself, I found myself praying for you;
I forgot your 20 writers and set designers,
forgot your lines and excellent lighting
I forgot the dozen critics and the blogs,
the pre-release, the torrent, DTT.
I wanted you to be more real than me.

Binge

'Something we need to work on
is trying to get you to leave your phone
in a different room when you're watching TV,'
says Cain. 'Doing stuff on your phone
means you're not concentrating on the show,
and watching a show means
you're not writing anything coherent on your phone.
It ruins both activities — you might as well be dead.'

Sometimes Cain and I watch
so many episodes of something in a row
we get bedsores.
I drank so many nice beers I forgot how cheap normal beers were,
but now we have replaced quality with quantity
and we are much the better for it.

When we have watched enough episodes
I am allowed to get my phone
and I read reviews and commentaries on the episodes
and sometimes the sun comes up.

Cain splutters awake and glares at my face
picked out in white light.
'I think it's time I left or took drastic action
or something,' he says.

Cain Reverses Time

Cain's beard grows into Euclidean space:
its anchors catch on every form and drag them back.
He is a camera capacious enough to film the entire world
forever, and then rewound to unmake every wound.
I wait for it to stop once I am reunited with my family.
I fall asleep with my hand on her waist, our sons
on either side. I feel like an illustration on a jug.
But no. A suicide bomber is making a pasta collage.
He cries when his mum is the last one to pick him up.
A friend reverses all the way from the accident
to his last conversation about Tallis's *Lamentations*.
Nations slip inside nations like matryoshka dolls.
Oh, I see. I see what this is about. The fecund plains,
the scattered grain and oranges, almonds, passion fruit,
apples, berries, marrows, tomatoes, lychees
whip up and, in a reverse whirlwind, assemble neatly
on the grassy dais. But something is wrong.
Cain is not trying to reverse his decision, but God's.
An altar where a muscular lamb bleats ignored.
A shaft of light gutters, hesitates then settles in
to bathe Cain's offering in holy light. He
stands over his brother's body, a jawbone
in his fist, and we follow the drip of blood in, frankly,
melodramatic slow-motion. Thanks anyway.

BOOK II

THE ANAGRAMS

355 LETTERS

E	42
A	24
O	33
I	17
U	12
Y	6
T	41
N	23
S	13
H	41
R	26
D	19
L	10
M	7
C	7
F	6
W	6
G	5
P	2
B	9
V	4
K	2

And the Lord said unto Cain, Where is
Abel thy brother? And he said, I know not:
Am I my brother's keeper? And He said,
What hast thou done? the voice of thy
brother's blood crieth unto Me from the
ground. And now art thou cursed from
the earth, which hath opened her mouth to
receive thy brother's blood from thy hand;
When thou tillest the ground, it shall not
henceforth yield unto thee her strength; a
fugitive and a vagabond shalt thou be in
the earth.

Gen 4:9-12

i

After a busy Autumn pilot season, *Cain* was picked up by VQS (Value; Quality; Service) – a shopping channel specialising in charm bracelets, kitchen gadgets and compact exercise equipment – to add to their emerging portfolio of original programming, designed to take advantage of the lucrative post-box-set View on Demand market where binge-watching needn't even be interrupted by changing the disc. The pilot episode set up a familiar shooting gallery of sitcom tropes which barely prepared us for what was to follow. Two men rent a flat in a disputed territory, a city on the borderland between belligerent countries. The series was created by Mitchel Halberg and designed to fill the space between VQS's more traditional human interest drama *Confession* and the out-and-out slapstick of *A Swine Like Me*. Dr Otto Thud, VQS commissioner, was warned off working with Halberg, generally seen as a renegade by past collaborators. Halberg was script editor on four moderately successful shows for middling networks, he had been fired twice and walked out once. His work was well thought of for its off-kilter sensibility and its paving the way for more successful heirs to his style who somehow made it more commercially viable. At this point in his career, neither a celebrated veteran nor a rising star full of potential, nobody would touch him. "If Halberg could make a soap opera where the characters are doorknobs and a pneumatic drill constantly runs in the background, he'd do it," Thud recalls being told by Steve Nevers. "Keep firm hold of the leash." But Thud had faith in Halberg and his project and saw his role at VQS as bringing back a golden age of experimentation and patience, where artists are mentored and given time to unfold their ideas. It was his

> Cain and Father K. share a property. A hutch in the suburb of bachelorhood. Overhung by cheesecloth, shoehorned with mutton & things reabbreviated. The hairy household mythologist & his adherent undertow. Ornamentation: a hat, bunch of rhododendrons. Diadem the width of a yacht. Oh, seventeenth endowment. Don't try to thwart a stammered buffet. This, the trillionth interlude. The buttonhook will have his thread, the drogue, her logorrhea.

hope that the doomed show might evolve into a manner of "eerie drama/sitcom" with crossover potential for a mainstream audience weary of being patronised and eager to embrace stronger drink. At the very least he hoped allowing Halberg free-rein might create a cult classic, a 'showrunner's show' which might attract other ambitious writers to work for his channel. You will note that this is the hairy, bearded Cain of the Maciejowski Bible, Leaf 2. The actor portraying Father K was to change between the pilot and second episode, the point at which the season is considered to be strictly canonical. The writers were required to learn several new words during the process due to the restrictions of the form, which we do our best to cover in these notes. A drogue parachute is the small initial parachute which inflates and draws out the main parachute. On a boat, the storm **drogue** is a similar looking device which keeps the boat steady during a tempest; a sort of funnel or water anchor. In this sense **logorrhea** (a communication disorder: to be excessively and largely nonsensically talkative) becomes the air or the sea. Maritime imagery pervades the first episode with the metaphorical undertow, the yacht used as a unit of measurement, the (in all likelihood) seafood buffet, a sort of drowning or inundation.

Bold, then, to follow this opening with the notorious "drunk episode", in which Father K remains in the bath, raving incoherently, for the duration. Usually the first person POV is Fr K himself (Halberg is on record as seeing Fr K as a kind of alter-ego / altar-ego) but here, rarely, it appears to be Cain, giving the viewer an alternative perspective on Fr K before the normative had been established. No doubt a misguided early outlier which must have put a percentage of the audience off before they'd really given the show its due chance, but for those willing to see the hour (plus ads) through, a number of pleasurable leitmotifs would emerge. Rewatching S1E2 now it's hard not to be struck by the claustrophobic bravado of the setting, all real action implied by sound effects. It was then, for a have this much audience: the to extensively history of the understand K's dialogue, for feels radical. refusal to take dances so close what reason? Fr already out of which cannot his "boyhood alone the chaos being committed flat with its

Father K. & Bourbon in the bathtub. Why, that escalated fast! Whenever he unhands it, he shivers. I say we are unthinkably connected. His retort: a wooded Tarot rant, third odour hushed with boyhood horrors. Never seen death that uncompetitive. Get uninterpreted blancmange, FWD: hearth light. Ah, rhombohedral monolith to the hundredth motherhood! Ah, tenth cheetah hemorrhaging by domed foothills! A cloud of flies, their toothy neurons out.

rare, even show-runner to respect for their need for viewers research the Tarot deck to even 2% of Fr example, still Death's utter Fr K even as he to the edge: for K's drinking is control, a vice even mute horrors", let and enormities outside the comforting

hearthlight. Even if "uninterpreted blancmange" was something of an in-joke, other references were far clearer. Something had already died, or was in the process of dying, nastily: the flies had anticipated the feast and gathered in advance. Cain here acts as both judge and interpreter, despairing of Fr K even as he remains utterly loyal. And if it feels odd now to see our protagonist playing the level-headed one, that's really testament to the show's ability to harness authentic character development. It was an early indication of the series' highlights; the writers tentatively feeling their way into their roles with the combination of apprehension and joy that marks a new relationship and, in that sense, all the better for it. We felt sure we'd be seeing more of the rhombohedral monolith and we weren't to be disappointed.

iii

Cain tended to break rules and saving the introduction of a principal character for episode 3 was the most significant early decision. Previously romantically associated with both Cain and Fr K, Adah had been away on a business trip for three months, returning to find diplomatic relations between her country and their bellicose neighbour in tatters. Staff writer James Ingram recalls the atmosphere in the room when they realised that the letters b, i, t, c, h, d, i, t, t, o were left over after Fr K's feverish definitions. "We just started opening windows and whooping at the world," he says. "It was character defining. This was Adah in her own words wresting control back from the first breath.

worked on since proudest of unlike the accident' of later 'In Which Cain (S1E23), we that the writers implications a coincidence. charged with a hysterical from the male and desires need to name names, to take her in some way specific way. an unabashed episode, albeit the corridor,

<Doorbell.> Adah in Burberry, bathed in hall-light. Adah, rosebud torturer, co-author of overset thermometers. Adah, outshining hydrogen trinketry. Soothe their wrathful orphanhood then come hither, nutrient. Heavyweight statuette. Handbook for flesh data & VAT theft; the lighthouse den where redemption inducts honey. Brunette A.D.D., ol' mouthwash. Adahhhh! Tetchy demon & conventional Frenchwoman. Death, wishbone, horseshoe.

'Ditto, bitch.'

idiot with her Whatever I've I'm probably that." Not famous 'B-minus season favourite Marks Me' may reflect now overlooked the of so terrifying The episode is sexual tension, joint-chorus leads, their hopes for Adah, their her with many ownership of or in one very Indeed there is eroticism to the set entirely in which saw early

accusations of gratuity. The show would grow accustomed to courting controversy in this way, occasionally falling foul of the Bechdel test (a scene cut from episode 12 featured Adah in conversation with herself about the two male leads for half an hour). Halberg remains impenitent. "Adah isn't just the love interest – that's exactly what we wanted to parody in this show. She's supposed to be the rudder, the only one with a handle on the situation who might do something about it. Of course Cain and Father K just spend the whole time drooling and lusting after her: they're imbeciles."

iv

It is generally believed that the writers had to make the most of a low budget and that this led to the grim determination of writing through restriction, bottle-episodes and constraints. In reality the show was generously bank-rolled by Otto Thud off the success of *Swine*, but several costly set-pieces had been planned which depleted the kitty. Nevertheless, episode four, comprising solely an intimate kitchen dialogue between Fr K and Adah, remains a fan favourite. "It was one of the last things we shot," recalls Halberg. "Kitty [Beaulieu, who plays Adah], had really

-Tell me again how you were defrocked.
-Overnight.
-That's half.
-Bibulously.
-That's hardly uncharacteristic.
-Alright. There are things we don't fathom: the 'noumenon'.
-That's better. Humour me.
-March 5th, The Hour of Botheration: the invertebrates trashed the transept, uprooted the boutonniere... This vermivorous, backhanded ordination...
-Wood!
-Bonded, drowned hobo.
-Oh, Eden! Oh, heeded ode!
-And faith?
-N-No, th- th... H- h- h- h- h- h- h-
-You're crying. Why?
-It's all that's left.

by then which as we wanted of previous talk They both had I got them to line so that it completely gives the scene personal as if you're own neighbours wall." Adah is find that in the she has been no longer has and privileges a cleric. To be be excessively alcohol which is, out, hardly Father K's line of further. Father off by talking philosophy (the posited thing, which is known, at all, without senses), but it that a violent the church has

got into the role was important to imply years between them. contact mics and whisper every was almost inaudible. It that indecently atmosphere, overhearing your through the dismayed to three months away, Father K the obligations to function as *bibulous* is to fond of drinking as Adah points unusual for work. She probes K tries to fob her about Kantian *noumenon* is a object or event if it is known the use of the soon emerges overthrow of taken place,

the transept vandalised, Father K (and, we suppose, his ilk) booted out and replaced by patsies during The Hour of Botheration. Its having been *titled* shows that the recent event has already passed into myth – a further indication that there is no planned resistance. This augurs very ill, and the look on Adah's face as K sobs in her lap adequately communicates whatever the dialogue had missed. She realises that she will have to act as leader, as cheerleader, as mother, as father to the household.

This saw the beginning of the celebrated 'College Years' plot arc. There is no longer any work for Adah with the Foreign Office; the entire sector has been deemed unpatriotic. Father K is no longer recognised by the state, as established in episode 4, and Cain himself has always inhabited the role of the "zany friend" who seems to pay his way, but God only knows how. Thus it was a matter of time before the writers chose to exploit the fertile context of the local university, named for King Ethelred the Unready. It should be noted that "unready" is a mistranslation of an Old English word which might more accurately be rendered "ill-advised". The main

exposed masses batholith are the South West being rich in tin. is to render immune to a administering is named for VI, the son of king of Pontus father died of Mithridates VI that the same befall him that ingested tiny numerous toxic belief he might immunity. In the technique zookeepers or performers poisonous imagines they a little snake their tea every we can assume has some function: in a despicable

We enrol at HRH Ethelred University at Adah's behest. Cain has taken 10 evening modules:

Arsehole Theory; Misunderstanding 101; Heartburn Studies; The Novelette; Troubleshooting the Mithridatised; The Modern Underachiever; Draw in H, 2H, 3H, 4H, 5H, 6H, 7H, 8H & 9H (& Rub); Footnote Clutter; NSFW.

Father K:
Doubt; Hebrew; The Churchy Batholith; Bird Orthography; To Deflower The Footpath & Ha-Ha; Cottonmouth; Nonconformity; Downloaded Hoodoo.

Adah:
Threat; Bayonetting.

of the Cornubian responsible for of England Mithridatism yourself poison by self- tiny doses. It Mithridates Mithridates V, 150-120 BC. His poisoning and was so afraid fate might he constantly amounts of substances in the develop blanket the modern era may be used by circus/burlesque who work with animals. One might squirt venom into morning. Here the word also metaphorical order to accept or poisonous

ideology it may be necessary to agree with homeopathic amounts of it, i.e. "to go along to get along". To troubleshoot the mithraditised could be taken one of two ways depending on whether the mithradist in question is friend or foe. Both Cain and Father K revert to type here, taking evening classes which reinforce their deeply held views and confirm that which they hold to be self-evident. Only Adah, who understands the gravity of the situation, takes courses which might be of some use in the struggles to come. Always a fan favourite, Halberg grudgingly acknowledges this episode as a stand-out. "Fuckin' pencils," he adds. "You people are a constant disappointment."

vi

Whether The Lachrymator refers to Cain or Father K is unclear – neither emerges from this episode with much dignity. **Holothuria** refers to the genus of the seacucumber and Cain performed exquisitely here, bobbing around painfully slowly as if along the bottom of the ocean, at times barely moving at all. Adah's rendition of the house sledgehammer was noted at the time for its energy and, yes, bravery, and it is pleasing – or perhaps worrying –

Lethargy in knitwear, the drabbest thunder. Fr K. botches another investigation. The Corroborated Brotherhood of Hoods telephone: 'Have hashish? Not?' A tolbooth haberdasher hid by a eunuch at the threshold of the mine. Cain went in holothurian stupor, diverting the headway. Oh, M____f____. Had we overdosed on thought? TNT? *That?* The house sledgehammer rewound, cottonmouthed with fame, incredulity and The Lachrymator, his ferry untether'd, null.

to see that her
has stood the
had already
these characters
them turning
THC-induced
not a pleasant
a necessary one,"
us. "It's easy
limited most
the time by the
'relatable'
does 'relatable'
mean seeing
back at you,
Also we had a
which people
realise because
of the form. But
left us to it. If we
K to believe, for

performance
test of time. We
come to love
and seeing
on each other in
paranoia was
experience, "but
Ingram reminds
to forget how
series were at
need to feature
characters. What
mean? It doesn't
yourself reflected
that's for sure.
lot of freedom,
maybe don't
of the strictness
Otto pretty much
wanted Father
one episode that

he was an incompetent private detective, we wrote it. If we wanted the last ten minutes of the episode to show the house being smashed to pieces in reverse so that next week everything could be back to normal, that's what we did." We see a recursion of maritime imagery in the final moments, the untethered ferry, good for nothing, no means of escape.

Father K, at his creepiest, spends the entire episode hiding in Adah's wardrobe, waiting for her to come home. When she does we brilliantly only see a close up of his own wet eyes. Adah's original line was "You want your social disorder honoured as a *coup de theatre*" which is more rhythmically pleasing as well as more meaningful, but it was impossible to make it work with the letters available. In the end, and after two long nights, the writers admitted defeat and settled for **surrebutter**, a legal term and a less preferred synonym of "surrebuttal". A

surrebutter is
by a plaintiff
the defendant's
heart-breaking",
"James [Ingram]
way this makes
than the theatre
better nuance,'
all see he was
what it was like
sometimes."
own *coup de*
acquire a speech
at the crucial
realises she isn't
he only does
sympathy and
voyeurism, but
believe that the
psychosomatic,
genuine for the
pretends he was

Hid there, he beheld Adah highlighted in bicarbonate attention. A halo hovered over her headboard. 'The front! You'd have your social disorder honoured as a surrebutter: so much synthetic chutney.' Father K formed a thudden lithp. 'Thorry. T-Tenth, tenth.' Now he foments in her wardrobe, overwhelm'd. 'Hath to be thomething...' THC: The fluttering sonata's titillation.

'When the attaché shows us round the motherland, you ask one thing: How bombproof?'

the pleading
in response to
rebuttal. "It was
Lin Tseng recalls.
was all, 'No, in a
more sense
thing – it has a
but we could
crestfallen. That's
working on *Cain*
Father K's
theatre is to
impediment
moment Adah
alone. Perhaps
this to win her
distract from his
we are given to
symptoms, if
are at least
time being. He
just looking for

something (and maybe he was: one popular fan theory casts Father K as a double-agent throughout, converted rather than defrocked and working secretly throughout to undermine his companions). Adah, lying on her bed to remove her nail polish, is unmoved. She gives him some advice which has been the subject of no little dispute among critics. In fact it was a question Adah herself often found herself asking in her professional life: *What a beautiful hotel – is this where we'll be staying? How bombproof is it?*

viii

Viewers complained of a smell of molten plastic during this episode, brushed off by producers as a meaningless coincidence until a junior intern noticed it too on the rec room screen. She worked out that a light-spectrum colour combination of Adah's dress, the classrooms' intelligent whiteboards and the school's white marble obelisk bathed in sunlight through the dormer windows (the college's murals and installation art pieces are themselves the subject of much interpretation, seemingly hinting at a massive – and desirable – reduction in the global population) caused certain models of television to overheat. It is generally agreed that the college became a microcosm of the country itself, and episode eight saw Cain in a chrysalis of dissatisfaction, taught by the mediocre, soon to emerge as a revolutionary leader. It was the novelist David Markson who famously accused his own critics of being, 'at best, C students'. To **obnubilate** is to cover or darken, as if with a cloud, as one might their true intentions. Nietzsche's **tarantulas** have "secret ambitions to be tyrants", but couch their ambitions in

> He sees through the whole charade:
> Hereditary C-students running the show,
> without honour, beslobbered with awards.
> At mid-term they fail the truth; they hate
> both grammar & rhetoric. Hobbyhorse
> petitions have nothing on defiance; The
> Devoted of HRH hold to no dud Ark
> nor Whatnot's tarantula. Bedeviling isn't
> censorship (TL/DR). From trend-dotted
> motherhood, they huff on the hookah,
> their vehemence obnubilated. Hey-ho:
> natural anacolutha.

terms of justice mean revenge). all in whom to punish is hangman and look out of their all who talk justice! Verily, more than honey. call themselves the just, do they would be they had power." didn't read) late 90s and came usage in the Often seen on (and, later, social passionate

(by which they "Mistrust the impulse powerful [...] the the bloodhound faces. Mistrust much of their their souls lack And when they the good and not forget that Pharisees, if only TL/DR (too long, originates in the into common early 2000s. message boards networks) during debate. Should

someone provide a lengthy, nuanced, intelligent and even-handed post, > 500 words, it could be relied upon that the first comment under theirs would be a raspberry of this kind, from a friend or over-familiar stranger. The juxtaposition of the sincere, thoughtful and hard-won account with a deliberately boorish put-down never failed to raise a smile. Bathos or self-deprecating satire, it is unlikely that it was ever used seriously (i.e. the objective reader is not supposed to believe that the poster of TL/DR is truly incapable/lazy, nor that they genuinely didn't read the post; rather that they read it and felt confident in dismissing it: You know X, always going off on one / I might have put it more succinctly / this is just angels on the head of a pin stuff. Alternatively it could be a very necessary deflation when the truth, such as it is, may be simpler, but any one of these usages could be put to nefarious ends on the level of the social ("cyber-bullying") or the political ("propaganda"). It is very hard to say.

Episode 9, 'The Handbook and the Deviation', took a more traditional narrative approach such that regular viewers wondered if they weren't watching a different show altogether. Directed by Vern Lloyd (who would go onto helm the underrated episode 16 as well as taking up three uncredited stints as assistant later in the series),

In which the gang get the better of their lecturers and become the New Intellectuals. Fr. K hammers a bloodstained shorthand manifesto to the hardwood. "Harbourers: old guard / doubt. Both yoghurt." Victory is effortless: a dachshund thrown into the heather. Shoehorn in a few hourly untruths, the odd hot photo, maroon orbit, hymn the hip, heal rhyme, unearth the hatchet then… we're done. Avidity in the boulevard. The Handbook and the Deviation.

Cain took us into with the pace police Lloyd's past similarly instalments of *Bestiary with* and *Samson, Samsong* and this experience gang's essentially takeover of Appropriately, Cain's command, memo. Even doubts – let who protect a bloodless coup of a commercial procedural. credits include outlying cult favourites, *Floral Additions Samsung,* he brought to bear on the unopposed HRH Ethelred. it is Father K, at who sends the those who nurse alone those the overthrown authorities – are enemies, although it is currently unclear whether " yoghurt" is an insult, a threat, or both. Only Cain sits, pensive and troubled, while fireworks are let off in the grassy quad, Father K gives his first impromptu lecture to some bright young things and Adah draws up the new syllabus.

New Bloodtypes:

Aesthetic
Dishonourable
Shorthorn
Traditional
Hairsbreadth
Southbound
Ahhhhhhhhh!
Dehydrated
Retrovert
King (The)
Overstretched
Untrustworthy
Ghosthood
Inhabited
Roman
Thermonuclear
Fourteenth
High

Defenestrated
Thinkable
Honey'd
Chloroform
Theologian
Behemoth
Eden
Whitewash
Attenuated
Thermodynamic
Adventitious
Overthrow
Hypothetical
Foreshadowing
Unmatchable
Toffee (n)
Unutterable

One of several notorious "list" episodes, building on the success of S1E5, but stripping away the pleasures of story, humour and, arguably, juxtaposition. Only the most ornery acolyte would defend 'New Bloodtypes' against the charge of aggressive minimalism (Adah, in black and white, delivers the list while Cain interpolates for 45 minutes), but it did the sad job of crushing the idealism and optimism of the previous week, and we were left wondering whether *plot itself* wasn't a kind of obnubilation: a gorgeous mosaic of hype and misinformation. The gang divide the population into 35 distinct castes by bloodtype, each of whom are turned against the others in a maddeningly complex web of duties and privileges.

Dissension within their own freshly established elite was portrayed by a play within a play, staged by Father K for Cain's birthday party and cast with better-looking lookalikes from the Honey'd bloodline. The form was chosen out of many mooted (a musical, a dance piece, poetry recital, silent film, all trialled on the sound-stage but rejected for their mere novelty). "We wanted to do something which echoed Alfred Jarry's *Pere Ubu*," recalls Tseng. "It had to have the proper application and feel of the Pataphysical." Ingram provides further insight here: "Once it

Lin spent a
everything Jarry
including
the journals,
articles had been
Halberg casually
that he couldn't
and regarded
'total garbage'.
she was pretty
Halberg was
shit like that."
have Father K,
of the script,
by the same
restrictions the
faced makes
more immersive
solutions are as
and daft as those
the real writer's
himself dead
one-word line.
the king so that
may use up a
had a line of 41
my upper arm
says Tseng), he
trips over his

A double kitchen, unventilated.

CAIN: Hive the territories tighter.
ADAH: How do we reign?
CAIN: Through obviousness.
FR. K.: Autonomously.
CAIN: That toot will be your only line, wretch! *[Slays him.]*
H.R.H.: Fab. Art thou happy? Mm?
ADAH: No. Th- Thou?
H.R.H.: More than this tic bulb degenerate browbeaten horridly earthward. Or than--
ADAH: Cheat!
H.R.H: Outvoted, underdressed offender, hormone offshoot. *[He teethes.]* Th- th- th- th- th- the doghood dethronement. Best end-

[End.]

was suggested,
week reading
had ever written,
the letters,
whatever
translated, before
let it be known
stand Jarry
Pataphysics
Looking back
cool about it.
always pulling
The decision to
putative author
hamstrung
linguistic
screenwriters
this one of the
episodes, and his
equal parts deft
attempted in
room. He writes
after a single,
Cain is crowned
his designation
few stray Hs. ("I
Hs tattooed on
by this point,"
then anxiously
words in what

might otherwise have been a passionate final speech. "We realised fairly quickly that one of the easiest and most enjoyable things to come up were insults," says Ingram. "But maybe that says more about us than the nature of anagrams per se." The image of a debauched Father K as an engorged tic flicked onto the floor and squashed (we recall that this is an insult written for Cain to apply to Father K by Father K himself) proved an enduring one. Adah, once again, attempts to act as the voice of reason to Cain's megalomania. Cain as cheat would rear his head again in the road sonnet.

Generally regarded as a mis-step, this episode sought to parody cast-changes and unconvincing accents, and perhaps draw a comparison with other phenomena an "audience" is expected to swallow; to keep suspending disbelief as if nothing had changed. However, in this case Kitty Beaulieu continued to portray Adah, as she had since episode 3, so it is difficult to see how or why the audience was supposed to accept that the actress had changed. Watching now I can see that Beaulieu attempts to exaggerate the suspicion of an English accent which has always been lurking in Adah's voice, but this is charitable. Halberg bristles when this is put to him. "The whole idea of a mis-step... I mean were you paying any attention at all? You think this is a dance. People still come to me talking about episode X, Y, Z being an outlier. *Every* episode is an outlier. We did our very best not to establish

bit about turning was actually a members of the eat meat again years abstention. the flawed problematic sexuality, powerful for becomes blatant that Adah will no Cain or Father of gratuitous (which may sexual fantasies of the male The lingering cobwebbed

> Following which, Adah is recast as an English herbivore. (This budget shows where terminist priorities lie.) She won't hitchike with Cain / deadhead K's cotton shrine. C.f.: vend 'Ohh... Ohh... Ohhh... [Oath]...' or rhythm. Her bayonet mothballed under the bathrobe. Our tenderfoot undergraduate's martyred to adulthood. 4th blue bottle of hard vermouth by the hearthrug; the homophone attendant too, unfortunately. 'Dude, thy enchantment annotated forever.'

anything." The vegetarian reference to two cast starting to after over ten Even allowing logic, there are issues here: heretofore more its insinuation, when we realise longer sleep with K via a series flashbacks yet prove to be on the part protagonists). shot of her dusty, bayonet said

as much (and perhaps more than the writers thought). A parenthetical hint at the show's cancellation and the reference to the "budget" foreshadowed the unwise metafictional direction in which Halberg was soon to lead *Cain*. It contains, at least, one of the most florid descriptions of a fly crawling over a bottle of fortified wine, shot in three days and dominating the last fourteen minutes. Vermouth: The mixer turned mainstay. Ingram, on record as calling this his least favourite episode, has nothing to add to the last line. Way to kill a gag by explaining it. When you buy a second-hand book you are generally looking for a clean copy, unsullied by dunderheaded schoolboy marginalia, c.f. *oiseaux*; how else is it to work its magic? For me, even though others place it later, this will always be the moment where *Cain* started to unravel.

xiii

But not before several undisputed stone-cold classics. This is why we keep writing about *Cain*: for all its self-indulgent flaws it just gets it so *right* sometimes. Every standard element is here: the gang are still drinking far too many cocktails in one sitting, Cain is a hypocrite, Adah exists only to be interpreted by the men, Father K is so borderline incoherent you almost wonder if he's a malfunctioning robot. So what's changed? I think it's the widening of the lens, the micro to the macro. By this point they've all pretty much given up on their evening

Cain, though broadsheet in dialogue, harbours tabloid thoughts. A doughnut of prurience. I had Adah misconstrued (5th/6th Manhattan). T/K: Her worth, her 'no tent' theme. The red toothbrush threshing deconsecrated earth, boycotted labyrinths. Hot thin chef, overworked antihero of the bathysphere, I need you to be yourself today. Thoth went, font-born, on farmland. The mortar swivelled on the hill. Demilitarised, huh? Oh how vehement, Heavenward.

classes, walking
the university
and took over,
with a useless
of directors.
can look, once
is happening
and it's not
demilitarised,
stands to confirm
of word as
is grinding
Reasoning with
or unofficial
like attempting
field with a
overworked
produced
delicious and,

away from
they overthrew
leaving it in ruins
puppet-board
This means we
again, at what
to their city,
good. Officially
but this only
the emptiness
bond. Everyone
their teeth.
the recognised
authorities is
to plough a
toothbrush. The
chef had finally
something
this week at

least, it was a labyrinth we didn't want to boycott. **T/K** is journalistic shorthand for "to come", indicating a forthcoming addition to the text. (TK is a rare formation of letters and therefore would not be confused with continuous language as "to come" might). **Thoth**, one of the gods of the Egyptian pantheon, has either an ibis or a baboon head. Arbitrator of disputes between other gods and the system of writing.

•

Halberg poached one of the principal staff writers from *The Wind Might Change* for this episode and J. C. Meagher's fingerprints are all over it, from the domestic detail to the well-aimed hosepipe. There is an uneasy humour to proceedings as the slapstick and exquisite timing give way to a casual and brutal order. Persecution of the educated middle classes in the name of anti-intellectualism is hardly a singularity, but this upheaval

was to spare of television teachers, accountants, by all for it). Why? know," says a victim too. I what they could distract us from. was the best, by show she works gold." Cain, who arrange (useless) given little is probably Adah's ability a telethon is impressive in the a hopeless attempt to struggle and popular opinion favour it may sure put on a When Father K,

The Don-hunt starts: They throw a birdbath through the French windows, a retributory abduction, a voucher for generational ennui. Fr K scorched in effigy at the hall. 'Brethren...'

Hose: H_2O H_2O H_2O H_2O H_2O H_2O

The odd Twittered tenet, the odd hit, *troth Buddha*. Cain hails a hansom which hesitates obediently (Hurry!) Adah holds the telethon. Motto: unnerved v. outnumbered. The vote: oh... Slaughter? (Nod). Writers retort: Hmm. *Please like my fanpage*. Abandon home.

the creators shows (doctors, academics and contrast, were "I don't even Halberg. "I'm don't even know be trying to J. C. Meagher the way. Every on turns to appears only to transport, is to do, which deliberate. to organise genuinely circumstances: valedictory reframe the turn the tide of back in their be, but she can song and dance. still sore from

his symbolic immolation, realises their beloved Mr Buckles has turned the other acts against them, his reaction is more wistful than angry. A sorry turning point. It's always a pleasure to see Meagher's self-loathing actualised on screen, and of course writers come off badly, as they do in many of her credited episodes on her own show. The whole of *Cain* was pretty down on writers too, come to think of it; a worldwide coven of narcissists self-diagnosing as empaths.

xv

The actual mid-season report was a good deal more positive: Dr Otto Thud, the show's handler, was delighted with the results of the creative freedom he'd granted Halberg and his team, and the slow-burning success *Cain* was proving to be via streaming services and in Europe. "People were watching it just to see what we'd let Halberg get away with next," he said in a rare interview, granted three years after the show's final episode. The team recalls him fondly. "Otto dropped by the writer's room once in a while, and really he was just like one of us," says Tseng. "We knew he'd stood by the show when others were attacking it, we knew he'd defended it to the paymasters.

enthused and
we were building
might actually
here – and in
culture that's
to have Halberg
this was really
than a little too
itself. Even now
episode 15
a perverse
the hand that
because. Either
the boundaries
or a teenager
according
combination of
was portrayed
unflatteringly
delivered such
demands as
character who
of the remit
Furthermore,
this is where a
of the audience
The show had
them already,

E-PORT FROM THE D.H. (HD, 3D) 34T67:

We like the brother. Can we bring the brother in again?

Suggestions: horror, bromance, homeopathic subordination, D.T.s, death.

Strengths and threat: Father K. is a duodenum - he absorbs irony. Ohhhhhhh! This means both.

The verve is currently outdated, the decathlon a collaboration with the laundrywoman (heh heh heh!). You're heedful how the unlovely detente = duff.

What of theatricality? Voodoo? Entertainment?

- Dr Otto Thud

And he kept us
convinced that
something which
be important
a disposable
meaningful. So
turn on him like
upsetting." More
pleased with
the infamous
looks like such
act of biting
feeds you *just*
that or to test
like a toddler
(Halberg being,
to Ingram, a
the two). Thud
by an actor,
cast, and
unreasonable
the return of a
died outside
of the show.
ratings-wise,
good proportion
checked out.
asked a lot of
and they were

understandably wary of metafiction. Halberg is, of course, unrepentant. "Do you know why people dislike metafiction? It's not because it's boring or done before or not-as-clever-as-it-thinks or whatever they tell you. It's because it terrifies them. And yes, it had to be Otto. If I wanted people to believe the show was really in trouble, if I wanted to actually place the show in jeopardy, which I *did*, it had to be Otto's name. Yes, it hurt his feelings, that was my intention. I was making a film about people being displaced. This is Total Art. If you cannot see the parallels, I feel sorry for you."

xvi

Remembered chiefly for the driver's snore, this was Vern Lloyd [director of episode 9]'s second run as director and I've always considered it the perfect miniature road movie. Everything just made so much sense here; Ingram and Tseng delivered a script with few obscure words or contortions of plot and Lloyd was only too happy to shoot it as the afternoon sun gave way to a sultry August evening. The gang bounce the tarp in a flatbed truck full of watermelons. Cain tries to read the paper but only picks up the odd deeply upsetting word. The driver's name, Toto, is of course that of the dog from *The Wizard of Oz* (portrayed in 1939 by Terry, a female Cairn Terrier who featured in 16 other films but was only credited in *Wizard*, and even that was as Toto rather than Terry). "Toto, I've a feeling we're not in Kansas anymore": an inevitable echo of some boundary, literal or otherwise, having been crossed. A spot-check turns out to be Toto taking a nap and our three heroes urinate in a wheatfield.

They are crushed by the watermelons, thumped over potholes and downed lines. One wheel hics on its hinge with each corner. Cain cannot read The Times, the word *...bloodbath... ...interrogation... ...turnaround... bodyguard...* THUD!

Huh? A mandatory break. Toto? Toto? Buddy? *Toto?* Too hot,

the driver's arms dangle, butt odour, his mouth slack: *Hnhhhharrrrhhhhhhhfff.* They hotfoot to relieve themselves in the wheatfield then hibernate again beneath the fruit.

That's literally it, and sometimes that's all that's required. The solemn pace and lack of any on-screen drama gave the episode a dusky, muted quality wherein it was easy to share the protagonists' grief for their lost home as well as their profound relief at having escaped it. .

xvii

It would be two episodes before the gang arrived at their destination and Halberg was keen to stress the length of the arduous journey. Therefore the remaining audience were treated to two solid hours of Cain, Father K and Adah playing word games to amuse one another and pass the time while the watermelons began to decompose in the heat.

both and acted ("Always a joy," In S1E17, Cain blurb for his own In archetypally **laevorotatory** optically active rotates the plane counterclockwise chase veers to counterclockwise). vengefully honest strengths and the series so far, beans and all, while failing to with more than genre inversion. pleasant that there at old formats; in age where a single cassette retailed tended to hold of entertainment, would be totally you even imagine?

Hi, another blurb:

"Cain thwarts further authoritative breakthroughs, at once hardened & unhewn, dated & forbidding. The chokeberry to overwhelm the Northbound doubters. Bah. (Ohhh, sodden hermeneutical dross bean.) The shootout: thematically intelligent. The chase: laevorotatory (hoh!). Furthermore, the enlightening 4D flowchart, the fermentation of the hard, impounded 2D 'today'.

VHS? How?

Don't heehaw: this shit outstays the honeymoon period."

Halberg directed as script editor mutters Ingram). comes up with a life (or own show?) convoluted fashion, refers to an substance that of polarised light (i.e. the car the left or runs The blurb is a account of the weaknesses of fermented dross smiting its enemies reward the faithful the occasional Nevertheless, it is is room to poke fun the not so distant commercial VHS at £13.99 and only 90 minutes a show like *Cain* impossible. Can Owning the whole

series would cost the consumer £433.96 and require a shelf the width of a living room. "We must have rewritten this, I don't know, thirty times?" says Tseng. "And it's still my least favourite episode by a country mile."

Another episode in transit. This time the gang experiment with the sonnet form to pass the time. It *almost* works, but I'm not prepared to let Halberg off the hook without a little analysis. He was on thin ice with the board by this point – they'd taken some convincing over the show's unusual 31 episode run and anything which might be considered filler went down badly. Otto Thud was a remarkable man and a preternaturally patient manager, but not a saint.

VESTIGIAL SONNET #13

Attenuator of the unknown runes,
Monthly portfolio manoeuvre.
A hanky held aloft to hired goons,
Hideouts tattooed somewhere in
    Hanover.
The childhood whitewash:
Shootable birthdays (2nd, 5th, 6th, 10th).
Enshrouded dartboard hum,
Her holohedral taciturnity.
The governable hatchet notifier
Shifts pentameter virus: coward!
Hatching horror, the dun battleground
Henceforth the absinthe dhow in HB.
My head besieged, my heart the
    trebuchet.

episode 15 must
effect on his
the dwindling
on grounds of
are given only
sonnet here,
to abandon the
rhyme scheme
the octet and
line early with
couplet (the
were never
More generous
have focused
drawn between
poets, between
economics and
while the poem
concerns Adah's
K's traumatic
use of alcohol to
Cain's inability
pentameter. A
vessel with one
this case a **dhow**
absinthe. This is
assignment Cain

The insult of
have had some
motivation to sell
audience share
pure art. We
one complete
which appears
Shakespearean
halfway through
finishes one
a botched
letter restrictions
more evident).
commentators
on the parallels
economists and
normative
poetic form, even
itself extrinsically
silence, Father
memories and
repress them and
to understand
dhow is a sailing
or more masts, in
transporting
in fact, the one
completed for his

evening class in pencil drawing. **Holohedral** refers to symmetry in crystals; to be holohedral is to have as many faces as is required for complete symmetry. Therefore to be holohedrally taciturn is perhaps to be reticent in as many ways possible as to maintain equilibrium. I mean don't ask me. Killer last line, though.

xix

Beautifully and moodily shot, this season highlight followed the most testing triptych in *Cain*'s history which jettisoned all but the zealots. I made some noise about this at the time, but happily the show enjoyed a small recovery as a boxset and via downloads – it would have been a tragedy for so few to witness what was clearly Halberg and his team's finest hour. The gang stagger from their truck blinking as if emerging from a cinema, but the real world to which they must reacclimatise is far stranger than the fictions they created en route. We belatedly return to the narrative point of view of Father K, which may account for Cain's sparse interjections being summarily shushed, but the padre was always the protagonist of the show, really, for better or worse, and *Cain* just makes more sense when he takes centre stage. The gang's former status still holds some sway in the slum and thanks to Cain's connections they are smuggled into the ruins of a stately home, temporarily safe, their journey far from over. This is no place to hide for more than a night – they are high profile fugitives and the territory is under enemy control. The street scenes stand out particularly. Makeshift living spaces have been erected in between every building and under this lighting they look like the spill of jewels encrusting a saint's skeleton. Valerie Barajas, who had directed episodes 5-7 returned at the height of her powers here (and looking at her previous credits it is clear that her collaboration with art director Max Shen was mutually beneficial). With her feature experience, Barajas was able to realise the vision drafted in the writer's room (this episode is credited solely to Lin Tseng) A **heteroclite** is an abnormal thing or person. The dictionary gives the following adjectival example: "the book suffers from the heteroclite and ill-fitting nature of its various elements."

> Starlight tabulates the ghetto. The roughshod cargo unmoor in a hotchpotch of incoherent 9-volt anarchists and hydrophobic suburbanites. A thorn-growth of tents between every house. We bribe the messiah with an honorarium and find our area: traditionalist - market; heteroclite - feedlot. Totter by the velodrome. Odd, not funny. Try the keyhole. 'That dolt nodded.' *Shhhhhhhhhh!* We huddle with Adah on the verandah of the unremembered ruin.

This made everybody unhappy. A call back to the false alarm of episode 17, only this time it *is* a spot-check and the fat zombie cherub – a former friend of Adah from her days in the Foreign Office – has sold them out to save himself. We'd been on the edge of our seats for 39 minutes before the inane, simpering chief found the single long blonde hair on the parcel shelf. I was almost in tears as he held it up to the baking sunlight before the cruelly timed fade to black and silent credits. It was clear something was wrong in the pre-credit sequence when

Adah, Cain and unceremoniously boot instead promised think it might perhaps), but by late – they had they had on of escape, and set my teeth of the show. though, that elicit such an response even bullshit it puts "You know or watch the and the feeling so inundated

Adah knows a guy to smuggle them through the "tolbooth" with all corroborant shibboleths and documentation. A fat, unwholesome revenant cherub. His dented Honda hollows their overdraft. Thirteen officers patrol the border. Their ode to contraband hit short, 'Uhhhhh, h-hey, David, over here...' The hundredth hunted benefit. The Modernist itinerant: they push the ceded boundary of what it means to emigrate. 'Why look, the country has a hernia!'

Father K were shoved into the of given their papers (naïve to be otherwise, then it was too spent everything this slim chance the sour note for the rest How fabulous, *Cain* can still emotional after all the you through. when you read news regularly when you're just with terrible,

terrible things and completely smothered to oblivion by everyone's opinions about them?" says Tseng. "And you feel calloused, as if nothing could ever touch you again, you're just going to be numbly nodding through other people's devastation for the rest of your life like you're in a bingo hall? Mass grave… immolation… sex trade… beheading… child abduction… FULL HOUSE!, right? But then you read one story, one little act of kindness in a lousy situation or one more dashed hope which kind of snicks past the roadblock and it just *breaks* you and you can't stop crying? That seems to be Halberg's M.O., anyway."

xxi

One of Halberg's more whimsical decisions: just when the action is coming to a head, attempt to pull off something formally innovative. "Underwritten? Lithe!" could have been a note to his detractors in this metaphorical on-screen corrections list. Each one of its 23 scenes was followed by a 'what really happened' reveal, until the audience ran out (even) of (false) hope. "It was a bold decision, and by bold I mean stupid," says Ingram. "I tried

him: if you go out from under 23 times they're bored and step think he had that trick in mind the table cloth cutlery, crockery undisturbed. over and over until the very smashes hell." The whole an unrealised them share a captors and K and Cain are together as the we jump-cut to and Father K as their hands their backs. After

Erratum:

For blubber, read brother. Compassion; shoeshine. Authoritative; whiten. Hard; daft. Veldt; thought. Inertia; inherit. Mothered; afterthought. Work; ho ho ho. Schoolteacher; orthodontist. Enlightened; muddy. Horny; hyphenated. Underwritten; lithe. Theft; fuddle. Honourable; anaesthetist. Handbag; ow. Thud; ahhhhh. Huh?; entertainment. Sainthood; elf. Revolution; neology. Dad; backbencher. Bosom; overstay. Watchmen; wretches. Hydrate; shoot.

to reason with to pull the rug somebody's feet just going to get off the rug. But I kind of conjuring where you pull out and leave the and glassware Only you do it again 22 times last tablecloth everything to episode was sneeze. We see joke with their Adah, Father allowed to stay sun rises. But no, their separation weeps hoarsely are tied behind an inappropriate

remark about Adah, Cain kicks an AK47 from the weaker looking patrolman's skinny arms and scatters the rest in a hail of bullets. But no, we jump-cut to Cain being repeatedly pistol-whipped by the same patrolman. It seems unnecessary to list the others. This is now a world where honour is an anaesthetic and the saint is as fictional as the elf. They beg for water. Cain takes a bullet to the knee.

xxii

Injured, sleep-deprived, sorely tested, Adah, Cain and Father K are falsely imprisoned in a shallow cave with other unfortunates seeking refuge from their war-torn homeland. It is hard to blame the writer's room if S1E22 'Unlike All Other Empires' felt as cynical and world-weary as its protagonists, Cain, in need of medical attention he will never receive for his infected gunshot wound, entertains the children with parables of the less than human. Father K and Adah portion out tiny fragments of dehydrated goat's cheese and dried bread found in a side pocket of K's

in some worn
the feeding of the
All hope seems
external point of
an unusually
half mad with
regards their
normal situation
And yet there
an ember which
been scotched.
the dust could
any ephemeral
could be the
the most
we possess.
bullshit. This is
planned to end
well aware that

Holed up in a bothy, Adah and Fr K share dried curd and stone-bread with the yet breathing. *Hew, chew, survive.* Cain: foulmouthed & hedgehoggy; not mint. The children have an illustrated book called *Dehumanise!* He reads to them. Afternoon: hot. Hot. Hot. Hot. Hot. Hot. Hot. Hot. *Ohhh.* Life hobbled, unornamented, unnoteworthy runoff. As Westerners-by-birthright it's hard to habituate to horror, huh? We try to leave some permanent scratches in the dirt.

deflated rucksack
out rendition of
five thousand.
lost and the only
view comes from
talkative guard,
sunstroke, who
plight as the
of humanity.
is a will to live,
has not quite
Those lines in
be as nihilistic as
gesture, or they
most hopeful,
human impulse
"Posterity is
where we always
it," says Halberg,
there were still a

full nine episodes to go in the projected 31-episode run, and that many shows could complete an entire plot-cycle without much more screen time than that which he'd set aside for the denouement. "It was discussed at the outset, so don't listen to Lin or James or any of the other whiners I should have let go at the halfway point." A toast to the not rescued. The Edward Said quotation in full: "Every empire, however, tells itself and the world that it is unlike all other empires, that its mission is not to plunder and control but to educate and liberate."

xxiii

A much needed swansong from Cain, blasting Father K's *bien pensant* ideology and everyone else in his path. A neo-liberal trying to ingratiate himself with the construction worker and trustafarian alike, his arguments lighter than air as a spectacle. aligns himself Russell's *The Superior Virtue* "Something redeeming in victimhood "And he's right, Ingram. "You them, but it's particularly *good* is it? There's take the side well-presented Otto Thud (who by Dr in spite phenomenology) unsought cameo

B-

"Fr K., you hater! The standard liberal monotony: thinking all that is persecuted must be the truth. Hah! But no. Some things are *only* persecuted. Oh Fido, thitherward, round the houses – hold the hardhat, hold the standby bandanna – you launch the featherweight countercharge, the mere badminton, the waterfront hotbed. Neon Ivy Federation! The moonlight fornicator: he had more worth. (*Hi, Dr Otto, where's the hooch?*) This is how behaviour devolved."

and performed Here Cain with Bertrand *Fallacy of the of the Oppressed*: morally the quality of itself" – Maliki. you know?" says feel sorry for not like they're or anything, a tendency to of the most suffering." Poor never went of his PhD in is given another as the moonlight

fornicator (a moniker based on an anecdote I cannot get anyone to tell me). Furthermore, "neon ivy federation" was generally taken to be a side-swipe at his beloved alma mater, [redacted], which Halberg considered one of the lesser liberal arts schools in the Ivy League. The last straw, by all accounts.

'A Scapegoat' kicked off the late trilogy ('A Scapegoat' / 'A Narcissist' / 'A TV Critic') which more or less saw the show taken off the air. Even if this episode made it appear that Halberg had almost become interested in story, the blame for the overall fiasco ought to be laid at his door. "I had nothing to do with episodes 24 through 26," says Tseng. "Ingram had just had a kid and decided to extend his paternity leave and I wasn't enjoying the new team Halberg had assembled, so I just left him to it. I had projects of my own." Tseng and Ingram would return for one episode each before *Cain* was cancelled. Actually 'A Scapegoat' contains many of the elements which made the show a kind of guilty displeasure in the first place: pace, vigour, comparative clarity and an impressive lack of ohhhhhhhs and ahhhhhhhs which marred its lower points. We were presented with another false-bottom, a little exhausting after the repeated switchbacks of three episodes previous. The "clap trap" of classical music where a movement seems to have ended, in this case plunging optimism into static.

It's him! Him! Having hothoused the eight-hundredth debauched, authoritarian baboon, the earth – thank heaven – hooves him out with a little help from the New Dust Theatre. The dotty rodent forerunner, tyranny's switchboard coordinator, Belial's subcontractor, *dragged from his bunker and hang'd!* (Hold the venue, Phoebe). Set: Troy. In thy teeth, "hero"! Huff on *that* cheroot, doorman! How's the deathshroud, honeydew? From here on all will be *[Static.]*

The despot has killed, the war over, and we will reach our in time... But close to frenzy only look as for our worst be confirmed. anecdotes of room under his little try-hard: than we should the last seven we had *Rest, toy* relate enough to the episode. First *try*, but toes try may have been

been found and is supposedly wonder if word heroes' captors the joy is a little and we need far as the title suspicions to Halberg's the writer's command are a "We spent longer have done over letters. Initially which didn't what else was in we thought *toes* to what? There something in the

deposed leader's toes trying to dig into the sand as he's dragged away, but I was wary of relying on the ellipsis. So we threw that out. *Tyres to...* but where? *Stye rot.* Gross. *Yes, Trot* or even *Ye Trots!* *Set: Troy* came to me in the editing suite, as in *game, set and match to Troy* rather than a stage direction." **Belial** was an early name for the devil, based on two Hebrew words meaning worthless or "without value". In one of the Dead Sea Scrolls, Belial is the leader of the Sons of Darkness: "You made Belial for the pit, angel of enmity; in dark[ness] is his [dom]ain, his counsel is to bring about wickedness and guilt. All the spirits of his lot are angels of destruction, they walk in the laws of darkness; towards it goes their only [de]sire." In *Paradise Lost*, Belial is one of the senior demons, cast out of heaven alongside Lucifer. **Phoebe**, one of the Titans in Greek mythology, was the grandmother of Apollo. St Phoebe, a deacon in the 1st century church, delivered Paul's letter to the Romans. Adah's wordless reaction to Phoebe's name, a former colleague at the Foreign Office who seems to have risen up the ranks of the new regime, was heart-rending to witness.

XXV

An extremely hubristic, unflattering and accurate self-portrait, this episode saw Halberg in direct conversation with Cain, questioning his own methods. The passing allusion to Pushkin's *Eugene Onegin* appears to reference Chapter 4, stanza XXXV: "But I myself read my bedizened / fancies, my rhythmic search for truth, / to nobody except a wizened / nanny, companion of my youth: / or, after some dull dinner's labour, / I buttonhole a wandering neighbour / and in a corner make him choke / on tragedy: but it's no joke, / when, utterly worn out by rhyming, / exhausted and done up, I take / a rambling walk beside my lake, / and duck get up; with instant timing / alarmed by my melodious lay, / they leave their shores and fly away." There is an unfathomable system of numbers within the show, which Halberg will not discuss, but episode 25 appears to be the key.

An **orthant** is a term referring *n*-dimensional analogue of a an octant (3D). has the feel of an / cuckoldry be a reference according to being the gradual horns. A **t-totum** is a little metal top used for William Ernest 'The Double Nothingness opens with the teetotum twirls, wax and wane

I could close the deal with my brattish co-author, harry reputation's toreador, or detonate the whole trenchant, unfathomable bandwidth. Thumb-horned orthant. (The bits where Pushkin's like: *UGHHHH! RHYMES!* and goes for a beer). Can't unread the footnote: Is this worthwhile? Am I? Oh shanghaied heartthrob, thirteenth dandy havoc-hound. Gentrify the favela runt or defend the loon; sod the chrome T-totum. Ever the bodybuilder, even in ghosthood.

a geometric to Euclidean space, the quadrant (2D) or "Thumb horned" order of mockery but may also to Cain's mark, some scholars, protrusion of (or teetotum) Roman spinning gambling. Henley's Ballade on the of Things' lines: "The big / And epochs / As chance

subsides or swirls…" Triskaidekaphobia can be traced back to the Zoroastrianism of ancient Persia where the 13th day of each new year is considered evil, or a day when the power of evil is particularly intense and can cause trouble, thus to this day people leave cities and camp overnight in the countryside. God has **thirteen** attributes of mercy according to Rabbinic commentary on the Torah, and thirteen is also the number of nodes which make up Metatron's Cube in Kabbalistic account. Metatron is an extraordinarily important angel in the apocryphal *Book of the Palaces*; it is suggested that Metatron is the only reason the human race was given knowledge of God and the cube forms a kind of 'map of creation'. This appears to relate back to the "rhombohedral monolith" of the early episodes, the college's strange obelisks. It is worth mentioning that Euclidean spaces generalise to higher dimensions. I feel really weird.

Who could forget that bastard robot – one of the most extraneous sidekicks since Scrappy Doo. He appeared beside Father K with no explanation, gibbering borderline nonsense and non-sequiturs from classic sitcoms. Maybe a fever-dream or mirage. You know, it only occurs to me now that this episode was taking aim at my own episode guides, written and published the same night as the original broadcast date. Mine specifically. Mine and mine alone. Yes, I may have been one of several dozen writers producing this kind of copy, but you'll forgive my taking it personally without thinking me paranoid: certain leitmotifs were unmistakably mine and I worked for one of the larger forums. I was told that lead writers on the show read the comments and maybe I thought they were mature enough, professional enough to take it on the chin. And so what? Did they think I was happy? Did they think I foresaw myself earning two pence a word churning out hackwork for an online cultural forum, raw meat for a hundred sociopathic commenters and a 23% market share of the television criticism sites which even bothered to cover *Cain* after episode 15? Did they think that was how I *wanted* to pay my alimony? Well, my conscience was and remains clear. This is

> All psychodrama bombards the fan with tortured plot-rhythm, but thus far Cain has suffered from hot-headed edits and eleventh-hour cast changes beyond the usual arbitration. Too hot to have H.D. leatherette, H.D. dinner. Adah, heretofore underused, came into her own in the hallucinated butchery. Reshoot the harlotry: a hit. Highlight: K's new gobshite robot - "Don't mention the rhombohedron!" Ho ho ho. (When void, return). The Entity giveth... We know.

the only thing I'm good at. It's the only thing I've ever been good at, so it really hurts me when you deliberately misconstrue what I'm doing for whatever self-serving reasons you have for wailing on a cultural commentator. Anything else is just Western essentialism, ersatz guilt at our own comfort and boredom. You think these are first world problems? Well go chew some maize pap. Do you not think people living in a warzone ever watch television and maybe read some commentary on it afterwards? You don't think they deserve that? You think people in the developing world don't have problems with their broadband occasionally? Well fuck Halberg, fuck *Cain* and fuck you too.

xxvii

A slow, meditative episode, largely wordless. Still imprisoned, still dying, still ignored, the gang can only speculate on the nature of home and exile, of persecution and the nature of evil. A **hougher** is "one who hamstrings cattle", as in one who cuts the tendons of someone else's cows or horses to hobble them, specifically one of a band of outlaws in the Republic of Ireland in 1709. Our response amounts to a repeated car horn. The problem, Cain avers, is that evil always has nature on its side, and always prevails because only evil can change the context of what it means to prevail. Your enemy may be unable to defeat you in a game of chess, but they can certainly kick over the occasional table and watch the pieces roll under the dresser. We should remember

that Cain has blood by now, portraying him put on weight production 26 and 27. The shied away engagement and its disapproval saying, "But can that anymore?" "Maybe it's best just in case everyone else without saying not saying actually they're ignorant. Maybe preaching to

'There is nowhere left, but if you had a home you'd walk around it restlessly anyhow.' Adah drops the mic *[thud]*. Hand-held debt, another handgun. Oh, Batman. Toothwort thriving on the great fundament. Evil wins because it sweeps the chessboard clear. The Hougher: their blade, their tithe, the tenth herd driven into. Truth, blandly: Hoot... hoot... hoot... hoot. Hindsight earthed for bereavement. Honour a broken form of one another. That is my torched church.

lost a lot of even if the actor had noticeably in the long interval between show never from political perhaps some of went without we really believe wonders Tseng. to say it anyway we're assuming thinks it goes because they're anything, but completely the choir needs more than

anyone else." Halberg was brought in as a fixer for the eleventh rewrite of an abandoned Batman feature film in the late 90s. He has spoken of the fad for constant 'reboots' of older franchises as "exactly what we deserve." He was, nonetheless, a fan of the Caped Crusader and kept a little bronze batman under the monitor in his office. "At one point Halberg wanted a passing reference to Batman in every episode of *Cain*," says Ingram, "some kind of Batman Code – but this was the only one to survive the editing process." Thanks to Adah we conclude on a note not so much of hope as defiance.

Halberg, the seasoned self-mythologiser, would claim that cancellation was his intention all along and maybe it is more enjoyable if we choose to believe him. This episode was shot as a documentary and there was some pleasure in seeing him turfed out of the office even for the least committed observer. In contrast (and in response) to the proxy mid-season report, Otto Thud delivered news of the show's termination in the form of a damning SWOT analysis (Strengths, Weaknesses, Opportunities, Threats) because he knew this to be the procedure which

Halberg the himself as a free- can predict what will be before it with, oh, You don't like How very and a minus every character, hours of reduced to a jibes, synonyms and grudging undercut. fact a character studio as a more which might show up after slump. The put in a lot of a novel-length Timothy, Adah's sweetheart, who excised from altogether in reference. decency had so thoroughly and Thud that

TERMINATION NOTE #78H41HH9H6 FROM DR. OTTO THUD (HoD, H.D.):

We are beyond concerned. Nothing has happened for 3 weeks. Oh yeah, "art". Viewers: < 0.2: bust.

Character notes:

ADAH = Adultery methadone.
+   -
ode without theft   bottled hate.

FATHER K. = Sourdough birdbath
+   -
neon rat   oohhhhhh... legion, heh heh! bat rev.

CAIN = Humerus shutdown.
+   -
hot oiled nude   narrative haemorrhoid

TIMOTHY = Yet to be used: wtf?

Strictly ™. No alternative channel rebirth, right? All of this belongs to us.

would irritate most. "He sees thinker, but you Halberg's view he's even formed 98% accuracy. business-speak? original." A plus column for twenty-seven meticulous work couple of glib for useless allowances Timothy was in suggested by the relatable outsider have picked the the mid-season writing team work creating backstory for childhood eventually was shooting scripts all but passing Level-headed broken down between Halberg the latter took

out numerous injunctions and exercised his right to ownership of the series he professed to despise. In case there was any doubt in the minds of the faithful that they might one day see their beloved Sourdough Birdbath, Adultery Methadone and Ode Without Theft ever again, Thud imposed the network's copyright over all characters, dialogue and story-world. Not in order to reboot at any point; purely out of spite. Halberg was given one more episode to tie everything up, and this he accomplished with typically perverse genius.

Rather than set up a synthetic cliff-hanger or cobble together a shock finale, Halberg opted for a bafflingly condensed collage of the 20 rejected episodes which would have seen *Cain* through to its conclusion under a more indulgent model of production and distribution than currently exists. Every previous director contributed and Ingram recalls each truncated scene taking as much work as a standard episode for a fraction of the screen time. Samantha

'Unneighbourly Vern Lloyd's Redhead' stand accomplished their own right alone in my that we will seven-episode a-series that of Surrender' VII. The plot more traditional with Cain, Adah rescued by rehabilitated, bar high-achieving Fr K becomes retrains as an marries Adah, for mayor. penthouse suite beautiful dark Cain learns to (he turns out to There are still the splintered were once of death and, found the action

Shelved Episodes:

30: White Theft, White Guilt, White Entitlement, White Tears, White Barbarity, White Voodoo

31: Thoughts On Alcohol and Manhood

32: The Horrified Chronographer

33: theft - bunny - brothel - bondage

34: No-No

35: A Moral Barbiturate OR The Haunted Redhead

36: Unneighbourly Constructs

37: Ohhh, Ohhh, Eden

38: The Untouchable's Handkerchief

39: Thank Statehood For That!

40th – 46th: Arc of Surrender

47: Advertisement - Lotto (HD)

48: A Handsomer Voyeur (HD)

49: Antisymmetry (HD)

Johnston's Constructs' and 'Haunted out as uniquely short films in and I can't be disappointment never see the full series-within- made up 'Arc parts I through takes a turn into sitcom territory and Father K British troops, a little PTSD – as city-dwellers. a bishop, Cain architect and who runs They share a at the top of a glass tower and play the piano be a natural). tensions between factions which united on pain in all honesty, I a little obscure

until the luxury apartment block is destroyed by helicopters and the three only just escape with their lives. Clues that all might not be as it seems proliferate through the final twenty minutes until it becomes clear that the entire trajectory is Cain's escape fantasy, moments from death.

The show remains, unshot. Adah rants. Cain bares his teeth. Starvation: a state without border. World without means. Haha. Who'd have thought. Total Interregnum. Theogony. Thrombotic idea. (Debt flogs verb). A retro daydream: I hid under the hollyhock. The prohibition-era nut cuffed me. *Shoddy fate, old horse.* To genuflect? Ohhhhhhhhh no... Vulture Count: Then. Then. Then. Then.

Noon throbbed resplendently.

Baby... I... tried... to make... the... word...

I reached for her.

xxxi

Oh, that Thou teach even me. I who abhor
truth, the stubborn bloodhound. Worth
three hairbrushes, if that. No: hydrogenated
fats. No: enhanced formaldehyde. What
shorthand thunderbolt could halt my
hibernation & dog thirsts? The unabridged
refrigerator, the unnoted cheeseboard. Heh.
Shortlist me with the redundant heathen,
half my covenant with toothache. Foot the
noun. Whatever it takes. Lord, have mercy.
Gospodi pomiliu. Kyrie eleison.

BOOK III
DEATH SHROUD

Cain's Waiters

Here comes Cain, over the brow of Istnichtvorhandenstrasse.

He's walked through all the blue fields,
two figures — *bowing?* — ahead of him
as if laying track for a cartoon train.

As he gets closer I realise they are waiters in black waistcoats.
One holds a peppermill the size of a bannister, grinding it before
        Cain's every step;
the other a tiny grater and a rock of parmesan, grating it in his path.

When he reaches my table the waiters stop in front of him.
The pepper and cheese collect on his brogues like a light fall of
        snow.

'What's with these two, Cain?'

'I never said when.'

Cheese looks hopeful.
'Did you say when?'
'No,' says Cain. 'Do you not understand the subjunctive mood?'
'I do not,' says cheese.
'So keep grating,' says Cain.

Cain and I Are Available for Corporate Events

We're just so happy to be holding your product
in the apple-thick quadrant
in the absolute centre parting of a man,

wrist tanline and a glass of water.
Nothing says disinterest like a photorealist.
Put that in your dream journal.

Nobody is happy when Cain swings by
with his attendant waiters, with his walrus balloon.
'Nothing dates worse than whimsy,' says the walrus balloon.

Everyone's cigarette has gone out
everyone's pilot light has gone out
so Cain tries to listen to my clarinet full of cement
so he tries to play my violin full of Xanax
so he tries to blow that trumpet full of wax
so he tries to play my piano full of sandwiches
he tries to strum my guitar full of brain.
It seems to mean, it seems to mean

something miraculous but so what:
the levitating pen lid.
You don't need to explain
a game called Juxtapotatoes:
Just put a potato next to something.
We'll figure out the rest.

The Author

In 1967 Cain killed the author.
This was a disaster for everyone.

Now language is a prison,
true communication is impossible,
our deepest desires remain eternally frustrated.

We are the flies nutting the closed window
next to the open window.

The mark of Cain is something thought disgusting
at a particular time in a particular culture for a particular reason.
Bring on the border-control puns,
the novel-length slurs, the other hands.

Our best efforts get edited down to silence;
I mean Biblical silence: the sound of a book with very thin pages
          closing.

Cain in Winter

First hoar-frost knocked off the last leaves
like a dog-shake,
the idiot said, but he was right:

now the branches are opinions
in ancient baskets
unravelled in excelsis

or upwards like someone
accidentally giving you the finger
over a pile of photocopies.

I've waited so long outside your office,
perfect-bound sisters of memory,
I got bored and went 'crazy'.

The missing screw knows the shelf,
the therapeutic use of self,

that pickpocket, trauma.

Interfaith Dialogue

The UK Islamic Mission has a stall outside the Bullring. We stop because they give my son a green Chupa Chups lolly and a Capri Sun. I hate the name Chupa Chups, but later I look it up and find that *chupar* is Spanish for suck and the company was founded by a Catalan, Enric Bernat, in 1958 after he saw a toddler eating a boiled sweet and getting in a terrible mess, the mother struggling to clean it up, and he thought, what if it was on a little white stick? His father's jam factory, which went on to become Chupa Chups Ltd., has an interesting history, emerging victoriously from the Franco regime to become the manufacturer of the world's most popular confection. Maybe I should write a sequence of poems about Chupa Chups instead. UKIM has some leaflets called The Real Meaning of Extremism, which feels like kind of a tough sell right now. They are also giving out free Qurans and I want to read the story of Cain and Abel in the Quran to compare it to the Bible. Apparently there's a great bit about a raven. I was going to buy one from Waterstones, but if I get a free one I save a fiver and we can have baguettes for lunch. Also, the Waterstones near the Bullring doesn't stock my books, so fuck them.

'This is free?' I say.

'Of course!'

I flick through the pages. Each chapter has suggested questions for applying the teachings to your day-to-day life. The translation is a little contemporary.

'Hmm,' I say, 'this reads like sort of a 'study' Quran. Is there, like, a King James Version?'

'A what?'

'I don't mean to be a snob,' I say, 'but the, uh, you know, the poetry of the language? I was sort of looking for...'

'What do you do, my friend? What is your livelihood?'

'I teach English at the university.'

'Ah, a learned man!'

'Well,' I look at my feet bashfully. 'Technically.'

'A man who appreciates poetry. And a man of faith?'

'Actually we're Old Calendarist Greek Orthodox. Even other Orthodox don't like us.'

'Well, you see we have beards like your Jesus.'

'Yes,' I say. 'They're really nice.'

'And if you are Christians, I have questions you could maybe help me with.'

The UK Islamic Mission rep next to him is less handsome and his English is less good. He keeps interjecting with *Do you have any questions about the Prophet? Do you have any questions about the Prophet?* even though I'm already having a conversation with his colleague.

I desperately try to come up with a polite question about the Prophet.

'I don't think so,' I say. 'But thanks.'

'Maybe you could explain this to me,' says the more Socratic rep. 'You know how to use a bucket?'

'Yeah, it's a thing, with a...' I say, 'with a handle and it's maybe made of plastic or tin and I guess you use it for carrying... In all honesty I've never actually *used* a bucket. There *is* a bucket in my garden and sometimes things go in it, but not intentionally. Just, like, some rubbish or leaves might fall in it or something.'

He tires of me and turns to my wife. 'Why does God need to become man to know what a man is? Do you know what a bucket is, sister?'

'Yes.'

'We don't need to *become* a bucket to know what a bucket is, do we?'

'He's got you there,' I say.

'I don't see the parallel.'

'But sister, you're an educated woman,' he says. 'So maybe you could tell me why that should be? We can understand everything about a bucket, we know exactly what it is, we use it. We do not need to become a bucket to appreciate any of that.'

'A man is more than a bucket,' says my wife.

'Touché!' I say, which annoys both of them.

My son has finished his Capri Sun and has started to cry.

'We're here every Saturday,' he says. He shakes my hand. He shakes her hand. He gives my son another Chupa Chups lolly. When we sit down for lunch I flip my free Quran to the chapter about Cain. There's a great bit about a raven.

Raven — A Text Adventure

You are swooping over a beautiful plane.
Everything is so, so wonderful
your tiny heart can hardly stand it.
> *land*
You land on the ground.
Two mounds lie to the east and to the west.
> *look mounds*
The mound to the east contains the charred carcass of a lamb;
the mound to the west contains a marrow, a sheaf of wheat,
some pieces of fruit.
It is, let's be honest, a bit shabby.
A shaft of light emanates from the mound to the east.
A dead body is here. A man is rending his garment.
> *i*
Inventory: you have: nothing.
You are a raven.
Do you want to scratch the ground?
> *scratch ground.*
Your claws rake the dirt.
This is the way you bury the dead.
> *look man*
You look at the man with your
darling little blackberry eyes,
with your beak like a conical drill.
> *speak man*
You make a sympathetic noise.

The man gets down on his hands and knees.
He begins scrabbling in the earth next to you.
Do you want to fly away?
> *fly away*

Genealogy

While researching the family tree, my father discovers that my great-great-great-uncles were murdered outside a pub in 19th century Cumbria. He prints me a long newspaper story with various accounts from different perspectives.

'Do you know what this means?' I say to Cain.

'That even your own family has been touched by murder,' says Cain. 'I'm very sorry.'

'No, no, no, I'll tell you what it means,' I say to Cain. 'It means I'm both more northern *and* more working class than my detractors.'

'*That's* what you take from it?' says Cain. 'Wow.'

'It's *very* marketable. I'm going to write whole cantos and sagas. Historical novels. Sad memoirs.'

'Like anyone's going to believe you.'

'I've got archive sources, birth certificates, multiple witness statements. What have they got? An accent?'

'Here's my review,' says Cain. '"To his delight, Kennard discovers that not one but *two* of his own ancestors were murdered. And if you think he's above using this as poetic grist to his poetic mill, prepare to be poetic disappointed."'

Shroud for William and Richard Jeffery

KIRKLAND, LAMPLUGH, 1871

Something you meant concealed by what you said:
it burned a little through the weeks ahead.
We didn't know of any bleeding then.
Cornish parents, émigrés to a small town
of ore miners, lead washers, blacksmiths.
William and Richard, in the off-hours, haunt their local.
This is the 19th century, so miners wear double-breasted suits,
waistcoats, pocketwatches: only it's all really, really dirty.
And everybody speaks pentameter or thereabouts.
Dick Leishman, 35, is stuffed into his attire like horsehair
in a wing-back chair; the bulging double-parentheses
of his arms, the genes we mostly lost in WW1.
The Jeffrys, 19 and 22, are in the mines six days a week
but willowy in comparison. Well-liked, as any
(a pub is based on fragile allegiances)
but it begins — you know this feeling too — when you realise
someone's been staring at you for some time.
It's him again. Dick Leishman.
Behaved nasty with you some time before.
I'm qualified to fight him and you too.
The younger strikes him and he strikes him back.
If you've seen a fight you'll know the silence
of a punch, all sound absorbed in scuffling feet.
I have the statements here like *Rashomon.*

Two pints a-piece, no dominoes, no games —
(the innkeeper is very keen to stress no dominoes)
and landlords read the early warning signs:
a thickness to the voice, the free jazz of chairs scraping,
flecked spittle: the initial drop of rain.
His wife takes the pots off the tables and sends them out.
Leishman has a room opposite the pub.
Dispatches one. *I'll fight your brother for five pounds.*
Quick, too. He strikes him with his right hand
then his left. He hits him with his foot about the knee.
The innkeeper's between them, Leishman towed away.
Will sits on the dykeside, damp seeping through his trousers,
his brother doubled up like a sack in a corner.
Hurts to breathe. Chapel window flashes the moonlight.
For a moment it's a scene depicted on a blue decorative plate:
Two Brawlers Lambent in a Ditch.
(Look at the inkwork on that drystone wall
beneath the smear of egg-yolk, which reminds me...)
Then it's a Blu-Ray copy of an HBO period-drama:
so many pixels you could swear you felt
the prickle on your neck and smelled the damp.
Inside a neighbour's house, the gramophone prickle of an open fire,
they ask him what the hell he thinks he's doing.
Leishman cries and says those are hard words when two set upon
        me.
His nose is bleeding and his arm is numb.
He says he wants to go and rip them up
then cries some more, and throws his blade into the grate —
it jacknifes with the pebble infantry;

a little pen-knife, a doll's sword
but just enough to jab a smile that spreads.
Leishman raves about gunpowder and shot,
says he'll kill the first bastard talks to him,
gets himself detained.
They didn't know of any bleeding then.
Will doesn't know it, but his ticket's punched.
It never feels the way you thought it would:
He kicked me right in the bottom of the belly.
It stings. They help them home.
You'll note there's no lack of samaritans.
Richard can go no further.
Only when the doctor comes — they cut his clothes
and find his bowels protruding from his side,
small lip, like the end of a tie sticking out between buttons —
do they think to check his brother.
By morning he's delirious, stopped making sense;
the basement window choked with brambles thick as snakes.
It's then Leishman returns, all sour smiles,
a man who can't resist a final word,
his voice the low rumble of a dragged urn:
I'll not disturb you, William, but I've witnesses to contradict you,
and to prove that you commenced with me.
We all live likewise, embroidering excuses
on excuses, weaving our own safety-nets,
death-shrouds until one day
our own murderer would like a word with us.